Kyle C.

How to Become A Great Business Analyst

Extended Edition

2024

Copyright © 2024 Kyle C.

All rights reserved. No content of this book may be reproduced and republished in any form and in any means without the permission in writing from the author of this book.

Author's Note and Revision update

Version 2.0

First of all, I would like to thank all the readers out there who have purchased my first book. I did not anticipate it to be receiving such popularity. This gave me all the support and encouragement for me to improve on the book with more contents from my own personal experience. I am glad that my previous version of this book offers some assistance to those who are working as business analysts in various organisations across the world.

The content of this book is revised to incorporate additional information, fixes, content updates and tips on the role of a Business Analyst due to the overwhelming support given in the first version.

I hope you find as much joy and inspiration in reading it as I did in writing it. Happy reading!

Introduction

I am writing this book because over the years of my career, many have approached me for advice on how to be a proper Business Analyst. Having worked in the IT industry for over 15 years in different roles, from being a developer, business analyst, project manager, product manager, head of RnD until I started my own IT business, I have come across all sorts of professionals with different attitudes, behaviour and skill sets over the course of my career. To be honest, many out there are not really qualified to handle the job as per their job title, especially in the fields of project management and business analysis. Therefore I felt there is a need to prepare some written notes to share with those who are keen to learn more about the role of a Business Analyst, or those who are interested to start their career in this path.

One of the topics that remained heatedly discussed was the role of a business analyst, apart from the project manager role within the company. If you come across any forums that discuss these roles, most likely you will find two camps in the discussions, with the developers complaining about these roles and whether they are really necessary in a project team setup; likewise, you will find the other team consisting of project managers and/or business analysts strongly defended their roles. The "technical camps" will argue that the development team would be much better without them since developers can also take up the job as well. However, I beg to differ, not as a supporter of the "BA/PM" camp. It is just that those developers still haven't worked with outstanding business analysts or project managers in their companies. If they have, they will be able to appreciate their work in untying all the knots and cleaning up the mess so the developers may focus on their task smoothly..

But in reality, we often hear bad things about the business analysts in the company. Sometimes you just can't blame them. I did come across very incompetent business analysts when I was a programmer, to the point that I was forced to take the mantle of that role to ensure that I could complete my tasks with fewer problems. Many would have agreed with me given that 78.2% of the respondents in a small survey that I did a few years back, said that they have no idea why a project requires a business analyst or what is the job function of a business analyst apart from being a messenger between the business units and the development teams.

First of all, we need to understand why this is happening and why I think every role is vital for the success of a project, including that of a Business Analyst.

What is a business analyst? What do they do?

When you are in an IT company or dealing with a software vendor to develop a system for your company, you would most likely come across someone with the job title, "Business Analyst", apart from the Project Manager that you will have to deal with throughout the progression of the project. Some might wonder, what is the role of a business analyst in the team? The project manager would take our requirements and then pass it to their developers to develop the system accordingly right? Well, yes, if you are dealing with a small IT company where the same staff has to juggle between different roles due to limited resources, or if the solution is just a small system or requires just some enhancements to the existing platform. When it comes to complex systems, the project manager will not be able to handle all the details of the business requirements, especially when it involves multiple stakeholders. This is where a business analyst will come in to fill in the gap and assist the project manager to deal with the various business users. A project team can have one project manager and multiple business analysts depending on the need and complexity of the project.

So what is the function of a Business Analyst exactly?

A business analyst's key role is to assist in identifying business areas that can be further improved to generate maximum business values to the organisation. The business analyst will usually review business processes, requirements and data gathered from the business users in order to propose changes that will increase the efficiency of business operations as well as to meet the business goals set by the top management, e.g. cost saving or digitalisation of business operations. The business analyst would work closely with the business units to define the business requirements that can then be converted into actionable items or tasks for the development team. In most cases, the business analyst is expected to review the business requirements from the business units and perform a feasibility study on them to form a "to-be" solution for the project.

Reality check:
A lot of business analysts would just take the business requirements from the business unit and pass it to the developers to start the development work, resulting in a system that is often riddled with bugs, requirement gaps, issues and features that did not completely meet the needs and expectations of the business users or customers.

If the business requirements given by the business units lack clarity, or creates possible conflict with the current business operations, the business analyst will have to bring forth the issues identified and discuss them with the business units before the requirements can be put into the documentation and pass it over to the next stage in a project. A business analyst is expected to perform his or her own research, seek clarifications from other departments, gather the market data, run data simulations or any activities required to counter propose better business requirements for the business units. There was a case at one of my projects where the business analyst would just "copy pasting" the requirements sent by the business unit into the requirement specification document without first vetting it through. Lucky for us, the document was reviewed and rejected by a senior business analyst. The requirements given from the business unit did not comply with the regulations and compliance for a financial system. If the unfiltered requirement was given to the development team and had it get launched to the public, the company could very well receive a hefty fine from not complying with the rules and regulations set by the authorities.

Once the business requirements is vetted and the proposal is ready, business analysts will have to work closely with various stakeholders, ranging from the top management who will usually be the project sponsors, to the development team that will build and deliver the solution, and the all business users who will be using the new solution or impacted by the new solution during roll out. This step is usually necessary for large scale systems where the changes to the existing system could hugely impact all other stakeholders or operation users. Usually the project manager would arrange for a project kick off session to explain the project to all the stakeholders while the business analyst would present the changes or explain the solution to the audience. After which, the stakeholders involved may raise or highlight any potential issues or impact to their units, and could provide some of the wish list to complement the features to the solution or system design.

After the project kick off session with the stakeholders, the business analyst will conduct requirement gathering workshops, interviews, and requirement gap analysis with business users to clarify any ambiguities. Additionally, the analyst will assist the project manager in prioritising these requirements, facilitating their inclusion in the project backlog based on their significance and business value. Typically, the business analyst acts as a key support for the project manager. While the project manager employs a top-down approach to ensure the project progresses smoothly and without impediments, the business analyst concentrates on ensuring the project is developed and delivered in alignment with stakeholders' expectations.

Once the solution has been delivered, the business analyst will have to go through the same cycle again to review the success of the solution and identify if there are any further improvements or changes required to the solution to achieve maximum business values. They are often the "go-to" person when the business users or developers are having questions regarding the solution, like an adhesive material glueing all parts together. Having a bad quality glue will see the project breaking apart as expected.

Tasks and responsibilities of a business analyst include:

- **Understand Business Models and Operations:** Gain a thorough understanding of the company's business modules and operational processes.

- **Identify and Prioritise Requirements:** Identify and prioritise both functional and technical requirements for the company.

- **Analyse Data Sets:** Analyse data sets to identify areas for improvement.

- **Conduct Interviews:** Conduct interviews with business users and key stakeholders to gather insights on their current pain points and issues.

- **Present Findings:** Present findings using charts, tables, and other elements of data visualisation to stakeholders.

- **Act as the Business Process Owner:** In some cases, business analysts will step in and act as the business process owner when proposing changes to existing business processes.

- **Monitor and Review Solutions:** Continuously monitor and review whether the delivered solution has met its business goals and objectives as intended.

- **Bridge Between Users and Developers:** Serve as a liaison between business users and developers by translating business requirements into actionable deliverables for the development team.

- **Provide Advisory Services:** Act as an advisor to business users, offering guidance on feasible approaches when requirements are impractical or contain overlooked use cases.

- **Maintain Documentation:** Create and maintain documentation, including requirement specifications, project sign-offs, delivery checklists, case studies, and other relevant materials.

Why Many Developers hated their business analyst and project managers

When you ask the developers this golden question, "Do you like working with your business analyst or project managers?" The answer given in most cases would be a resounding "No!" I have in fact carried out interviews with the development team in my previous jobs to understand this phenomena. From my survey, and my understanding of those people working in these roles, the key reasons why the developers hated these roles are mainly due to the incompetence of the people having these portfolios. Honestly, even I myself ended up in this situation when I was a developer and ended up taking the role of a business analyst because the business analyst did a lousy job at conveying business requirements to the development team for implementation.

Key reasons:

- Many Business Analysts out there do not have the required skills to perform their job properly.

- Bad communication skills, many of the business analysts are unable to convey clear and concise requirements and feedback to both sides of the teams.

- Setting ridiculous expectations without first consulting with the technical team before agreeing to the stakeholders, therefore setting the stage for requirement chaos and blame games in the future.

- Did not have the correct domain knowledge for the job to convince business users on alternative solutions, resulting in a "copy and paste" requirements from business users that might not be feasible for implementation.

More than 80% of the business analysts that I have come across in my career, be it within a company, or a vendor environment, sadly do not possess the necessary skills for their job, which is at an alarming rate. Many thought the Business Analyst role is easy. They just need to be a messenger transferring business requirements between the clients or stakeholders and the technical teams. Their only job is to deliver "whatever is being asked for" from the stakeholders and dump them to the developers to solve the problems and deliver the solution. The war or rift between the business analysts and the developers were also caused by developers looking down on the business analysts who are supposedly having adequate technical knowledge of system designs or basic programming skills. Unfortunately, those skills are often a statement on the CV in order to appear in the radar of the recruiters who might not be able to tell the difference from a piece of paper. They might even get lucky with the interviewers or hiring managers who did not ask probing questions on the technical side of things, and focusing entirely on the communication skills, "personality" and "attitude" of the interviewee vying to be a business analyst. Undeniably, having good communication skills is one of the key expertise that a business analyst should have, but basic knowledge on system design is important as well.

In the world of business analyst, you will find a lot of "rejects" from the development team, or even those IT graduates that are bad at programming will take on the Business Analyst job because for them, this is a cushy job and they can always find the developers to solve the "technical" problems for them. All they need to do is to suck up to their bosses and please the business users or stakeholders at the expense of the development team. This is why many developers still hated the "business analyst" til this day and feel they are a dead weight in the team. Hence, the long standing war between the BA and development team continues till this day.

More often than not, the bad business analysts have forgotten the crucial word in their job title, "Analyst". They failed to recognise that they are supposed to analyse the business requirements and filter them before passing them to the development team. Either they are lacking in common sense, bad at it or just didn't really care. This ultimately adds extra, unnecessary load on the developers' end. There was a case back then where the lead developer was so frustrated with the ambiguous requirements that lacked proper thoughts on the business use cases that he lashed out profanities in front of everyone in the office. I felt sorry for the lead developer as that was the fourth change demanded by the business analyst in a week; the third one was to revert back to the previous change, and now the developer had to add in more business rules in the software because certain use cases were not considered before by the business analyst before finalising the requirements for development.

Tips: This cycle of continuous adjustments and poorly communicated requirements not only hampers the development process but also reflects a deeper issue of misalignment and lack of effective communication between the business analysis and development teams.

Another significant issue with ineffective business analysts is their poor documentation. Many of them struggle to produce well-structured and clear documentation, which includes critical documents such as requirements specifications, tickets, user stories, and Functional Requirements Specifications (FRS).

In my experience, it's not uncommon to encounter business analysts who produce documents that lack clarity and precision. This deficiency can manifest in various ways: requirements documents might be too vague or incomplete; tickets might not provide enough detail for developers to work with; user stories might be poorly defined; and Functional Requirements Specifications that failed to capture the necessary business logic, scenarios and criteria.

Tips: The inadequacy of these documents can have cascading effects on the entire project. Without clear and comprehensive documentation, developers are left guessing about what is needed, which can lead to misinterpretations and errors. This not only slows down the development process but can also result in costly rework and delays. Effective documentation is crucial for ensuring that all stakeholders have a shared understanding of the requirements and that the final product meets the intended business needs. When business analysts fail in this regard, it creates significant obstacles for both the development team and the overall project success.

The good Business Analysts can provide documentation with clear Unified Modelling Language (UML) diagrams that will give everything that a developer needs to know to develop the systems. The flow diagram is complete with all the scenarios that are to be taken care of. Sadly, most business analysts now can't even provide basic flow diagrams for the developers to understand the business process flow. There are even odd balls who will write requirements as if they are writing the longest essay for the Guinness World Record; unnecessarily long and difficult to read. On the contrary, there were some business analysts who would give the simplest form of requirements in bullet points, leaving the rest up to the imagination of the developer who is unfortunate enough to be assigned with that development task. As a result of the subpar documentation provided by some business analysts, many developers found themselves having no choice but to step into a role they weren't originally intended to fill. Faced with inadequate or unclear requirements, developers often had to engage directly with stakeholders to clarify expectations and gather the necessary details for their work. This direct communication with the stakeholders, while sometimes necessary, is not an ideal or efficient solution. When developers are forced to bypass the business analyst and seek out requirements themselves, it creates several challenges, sometimes conflict with the business users or stakeholders.

Developers can sometimes be very blunt and reject any requirements that are deemed to be unfeasible or require big rework to the original systems. Business users, on the other hand, might be adamant on having those changes or features. To them, it is a technical issue that should be figured out and resolved by the development team.

The absence of clear requirements means that developers are left with numerous unanswered questions, scenarios that remain unaddressed, and use cases that are not fully defined. This lack of clarity can severely impact the quality and functionality of the final system, as developers may end up implementing solutions based on incomplete or misunderstood requirements. Furthermore, poorly defined requirements can lead to significant inefficiencies and is usually the main reason for the delay of the project. Developers might need to repeatedly redesign or overhaul their code to accommodate changes or fill in the gaps that should have been identified earlier in the process. This not only wastes valuable development time but also increases the risk of introducing errors or wrong expectations into the system. Many developers will eventually begin to question the value of having a business analyst on their team. When developers are already doing the work of gathering and clarifying requirements, they may perceive the business analyst role as redundant. Well, who wouldn't? This perception can undermine the intended role of the business analyst and lead to a lack of trust and collaboration between the development team and business analysis functions.

Since I understand too well on these issues, when I transitioned from a developer into a business analyst role, I knew what the development team needed most. In fact, I have taught other juniors how to be good business analysts which could help the development team to deliver a good work. Time is of the essence especially for projects with tight deadlines. Bad requirements will severely affect the progress and delivery of the project. When that happens, both the business analyst team and the development team will be locked in the dispute, blaming each other for the delay of the project. The project manager will end up have to resolve the disputes, but that will be the story of another day.

Fun fact: *The reason why I transitioned to the business analyst role was that I couldn't stand the bad user requirements given by the business analyst and ended up taking up that job to prepare my own documentations for my development team. I choose to remain as a business analyst as I could filter and prepare the requirements in such a way that the development team can work on the implementation with as little issues as possible.*

Tips: *Precise and well-thought-out requirements are key to the efficiency and success of the development process.*
A skilled business analyst can significantly enhance the effectiveness of a development team. Developers are experts in crafting robust and efficient codes to create high-quality software, much like how a surgeon excels in performing intricate surgeries. Their primary focus should be on coding and implementing solutions, just as a surgeon concentrates on performing procedures on the patients. To draw a parallel, consider that while surgeons may possess some knowledge about medical consultations, they typically rely on comprehensive and accurate information from physicians to

plan and execute surgeries effectively. Similarly, developers depend on business analysts to provide clear and well-structured requirements.

A proficient business analyst plays a crucial role in this process by meticulously reviewing and refining all user requirements. They compile these requirements into a coherent and actionable format, ensuring that developers receive precise expectations. This thorough preparation helps prevent miscommunications and misunderstandings that could lead to flawed implementations. Without this essential role, the development process can be likened to a botched surgery—where incomplete or inaccurate information can lead to significant setbacks, impacting the success of the project. In this scenario, a project might fail to meet its objectives, suffer from delays, or even be deemed a failure altogether. Therefore, having a competent business analyst is crucial for translating user needs into clear directives, allowing developers to focus on their expertise and contribute to a successful project outcome.

However, it is easier said than done.

What constitutes a good business analyst?

A good business analyst will need to be analytical, detailed, precise and decisive. These qualities can be obtained through experience and practice over the years. When preparing the requirement specifications for the developers, they would need to:

Understand clearly on the business requirements

What is the expected outcome from the solution? What are the stakeholders' expectations from it? Can the solution achieve what the stakeholders want? Will it solve the pain points? How to convert the business requirements into high impact, high value features in the solution, etc.

Business Analysts are tasked with identifying the critical issues outlined above to develop a proposal that effectively addresses stakeholder concerns and provides a clear solution for developers to implement. It is essential to avoid merely transferring the problems presented by stakeholders to the development team and expecting them to devise solutions independently. If you are currently engaging in this practice, it is highly recommended that you cease immediately and focus on thoroughly analysing the requirements. By doing so, you will significantly enhance the quality of your proposals and ensure that developers recognise and appreciate your efforts. Apart from that, you will be able to gain valuable knowledge on the industry practice, business scenarios and the value from the business requests. Failure to adopt this approach may result in diminished respect from developers and could lead to frequent disregard of your contributions.

To create a good requirement specification document, the business analyst will need to lay out the following:

- **Problem statement** - what are the problems that the stakeholders are encountering? The problem statement should precisely articulate the challenges that stakeholders are experiencing. This statement serves as the foundation for developing a solution, as it identifies the core issues that need to be addressed. It outlines the primary problem that the solution aims to resolve, establishes the goals and objectives for the solution, and defines the expectations of the customers. By clearly defining these elements, the problem statement guides the development of a targeted and effective solution that aligns with stakeholder needs and expectations.

- **Identify the problems in the current business process** - What are the current issues? What are the pain points in the current system? Which areas can be enhanced? What can we do to alleviate or resolve those pain points? These are the basis to form the solution design and feature list for the solution that will be delivered to the customers. The information will later be used as a measurement on how successful the solution is by checking the metrics before and after the solution is delivered to the customer.

- **Prepare a high level proposal with the new changes** - Once you have identified the pain points and have an idea on what can be done to address those issues, you can prepare a high level proposal involving some screenshots, process flow diagrams, use cases and share them with the stakeholders. This process might take a few iterations to root out all potential problems that might be overlooked during the initial discussion with the stakeholders. After a few rounds of discussions, you will be able to better understand their expectations, and at the same time, stakeholders will know the "to be" system that they are getting, which will definitely help with their problems.

- **Create those Flow Diagrams for easier understanding** - No one will have the time to read the entire description of the requirement in a wall of texts. A process flow diagram can easily help the developers to understand how the operation works. Apart from that, it is easier for the business analysts to identify use cases or scenarios that might be missing out from the business process, e.g. user might want to have a batch operation to process all the records in the excel sheet uploaded into the system, but how will the system handle if there is a record having data issues that will cause an error? A good flow diagram serves as a blueprint for the construction of the system. A good place to start learning would be those free online courses on UML diagrams, flow diagrams etc. There are a lot of free tools to help you with that as well, notably draw.io.

- **Requirements must be clear and concise** - Never leave room for the developers to start questioning the requirements. If they are throwing out a lot of questions that can be solved with common sense, then it is an obvious sign that the requirements are badly written and will create more problems during the development that will just be wasting the developers' time. They might have to refactor, revamp or rewrite pieces of codes later if the requirements are changed because some use cases are missed out or overlooked. This will just add to the development costs; more delays in the delivery, longer working hours and wasted effort. Therefore, developers will appreciate concise, clear requirements to be worked on. Having said that, nothing is perfect in this world. There are times where requirements could not be clearly defined even by the stakeholders. A good business analyst will need to identify these "landmines" and leave room for future enhancements, e.g. we can deliver a minimal but working feature/system and enhance them in later phases. The design must be easily extendable without much changes to the core feature or code, unless really required.

- **Be decisive** - Business analysts are required to be decisive when it comes to negotiating with the stakeholders. They need to have an understanding of what could be delivered, or rather what is feasible within the timeline for the project. They will need to set the cut off point on what can be delivered, what should be delivered and balance out the work required vs expectations from the stakeholders. Indecisiveness will only lead to scope creep, unrealistic expectations and additional work effort for the developers with no actual value delivered. Never be afraid to say "No" to the business users if they are demanding the impossible.

Quick tips to prepare a quick proposal

After identifying the pain points and formulating potential solutions, the next step is to prepare a high-level proposal that outlines the proposed changes. This proposal serves as a detailed plan for addressing the identified issues and should include the following components:

1. **Draft the High-Level Proposal:**

    ○ **Overview:** Provide a succinct summary of the proposed changes, including the goals and benefits of the solution. This overview should set the context for the detailed elements that follow.

2. **Include Visual Aids:**

    ○ **Screenshots:** Incorporate mockups or screenshots of the proposed user interface or system changes. These visuals help stakeholders visualise the new design and functionalities.

    ○ **Process Flow Diagrams:** Develop process flow diagrams to illustrate how the new system or changes will streamline workflows and address current pain points. These diagrams should clearly represent the flow of processes, interactions, and any new steps introduced by the solution.

    ○ **Use Cases:** Present use cases that describe how different users will interact with the system under the new design. Use cases should outline specific scenarios and demonstrate how the proposed solution resolves identified issues.

3. **Engage in Iterative Reviews:**

- **Initial Review:** Share the initial proposal with stakeholders to gather feedback. This stage may reveal overlooked issues or areas needing refinement.

- **Refinement:** Based on stakeholder feedback, refine the proposal to address any concerns or gaps. This may involve revising screenshots, adjusting process flow diagrams, or updating use cases.

- **Iterative Discussions:** Conduct multiple rounds of discussions with stakeholders to ensure all potential problems are addressed and expectations are aligned. This iterative process helps in fine-tuning the proposal to meet stakeholder needs more accurately.

4. **Align Expectations:**

    - **Clarify the "To-Be" System:** Ensure that stakeholders have a clear understanding of the proposed system or changes, including how it will improve upon the current process. This clarity helps in setting realistic expectations and ensures that stakeholders are informed about the enhancements and functionalities that will be delivered.

5. **Finalisation:**

- ○ **Approval:** Once all iterations are complete and stakeholders are satisfied with the proposal, finalise the document. Obtain formal approval to proceed with the implementation based on the agreed-upon changes.

By preparing a detailed high-level proposal and engaging in iterative reviews, you ensure that the proposed solution is well-defined, addresses stakeholder needs, and aligns with the expected outcomes.

"Business Analysts are the front line to understand what the customer needs; Developers are the builders to construct it; and business analysts will later have to deliver it to the customers. Having wrong expectations or requirements will screw up the entire process from start to the end."

How to create a good requirement that explains the issue and set the correct expectation from the business users?

I always recommend my juniors and other business analysts to develop a habit of creating user stories and then set the expectations that the team will need to deliver to the business users. A user story will explain why the user needs the requirement.

You can refer to the Agile SCRUM methodologies online for more details on how you can create good user stories for your developers.

Sample user story:

As the admin user, I would like to have an audit log so that I can track and trace all user activities in the system should there be cases that I will need to investigate.

From there, we know that there is a requirement from the business user to have an audit log function in the system. After this, the business analyst can start to create expectations and deliverables based on the requirement.

Keywords: *audit log page, track and trace all user activities, cases that warrant for investigations*

Naturally the system should be having a page that loads the user activity records and a search feature that allows the user to search the user activity when the user needs to perform investigations.

Expectations:

- System to provide an audit log page where it will load all the user activities captured in the system in this page.

- Users with the access rights will be able to search a user activity record by timestamp, module, activity type, username and email.

- The list will be in descending order; the latest record will be displayed on top of the list.

Note: The third item in the expectation list is a nice to have feature that improves the user experience. No one will be interested in looking at activities that had happened a long time ago, unless they need to dig out old records. That is where the search feature comes in handy.

If one of the requirements is too huge, it can be broken down into other stories for development later. This allows greater flexibility for the project manager to manage the deliverables to the business user, especially if the task is too big to be completed within the agreed time frame. Also having a good habit of breaking down the requirement in smaller bits will avoid scope creep to a certain extent, as compared to a brief requirement that carries much ambiguity.

From there onwards, the business analyst can create more user stories for each of the extended requirements above.

However, there are different ways to write business requirements depending on what works best for your organisation or development team.

Sample 2:

Feature:	Update Stock Quantity
Description:	The system must allow authorised users to update the stock quantity for any inventory item.
Input:	Item ID, New Stock Quantity
Output:	Confirmation message with updated stock quantity

Acceptance Criteria:	The stock quantity is updated in the system and reflects in the inventory report.

Sample 3:

Requirement

User will see the user login pass and will need to provide the correct username and passwords to login.

Business Rules:

1. Username - alphanumeric, 100 characters max
2. Password - 16 characters max, A combination of uppercase letters, lowercase letters, numbers, and symbols <list of special characters accepted>.
3. Negative scenario, if a user enters an invalid username or password, the system will display the error message *"Invalid username or password, please try again."*
4. Positive scenario, correct username and password entered successfully, system redirects the user to the main landing page (see section x.x for the main landing page requirement)

Additional Tips:

Requirements must always be clear and straight to the point. Business users should understand what they will be getting and developers should know what they need to accomplish.

Avoid one liners and ambiguous requirements such as:

System needs to have a login function for users to enter username and password to login.

Better to prepare the requirements like this:

System needs to provide the user authentication function for users to enter the username and password to login. If incorrect credentials are entered, the system will display the error message. Else, the user will login successfully into the system.

Avoid long, confusing requirements as if you are writing a best selling novel like the Game of Thrones.

Developers will know how to manage the error exception if wrong credentials are entered in the second requirement as compared to the first requirement. Business users will also know what to expect when they provide incorrect credentials. If the business analyst decides to go with the first requirement, the developer will not be handling that exception. All the business user will get when incorrect credentials are entered will be an empty page showing one message, "*An error has occurred*"

Reminder, again and again:

Never leave business users and developers alike guessing on the expectations. It is the job of the business analyst to analyst thoroughly all possible scenarios and use cases to complete the system design proposal. If there are requirements that are not feasible, the business analyst will have to raise it to the business users and negotiate for an alternative. Likewise, the business analyst will have to convince the developers of the business value of the requirements and provide a clear view to avoid any confusion. Otherwise it will lead to a scope creep as the business analyst will keep adding new requirements to address the use cases that were overlooked previously.

Diagrams are your closest friend

After setting the expectations on the business requirements and/or proposal, the business analyst can proceed to design the "To-be" solution. We will be using back the previous example or the the audit log page. The business analyst can use prototyping tools to prepare the visuals for the system so that the expectation can be easily conveyed and serve as the visual reference for the developer during the implementation. If there is a graphic designer team that can assist, then the business analyst can pass the task and focus on the process flow diagram. The combination of having the screen visuals, the process flow diagram and clear, concise description of the requirements are the formula of a good Functional Requirements Document that will enable business users to visualise the final product, while providing developers and the QA team with precise instructions on what needs to be delivered and tested.

Excellent tools for flow diagrams:

- Draw IO
- Microsoft Visio
- LucidCharts
- Microsoft Powerpoint (for simple flow diagrams)

Diagrams	Description/Usage

Start End	Symbols to signify the start and end points.
[rectangle]	Action/Step in the process. The step is written inside the box. Usually, only one arrow goes out of the box. *Tips: You can use colours to categorise system or user action*
[diamond]	Decision step. The question or fork option is written in the diamond. More than one arrow goes out of the diamond, each one showing the direction the process takes for a given answer, usually "Yes" or "No".
⟶	Direction of flow from one step or decision to another.

Sample diagram 1:

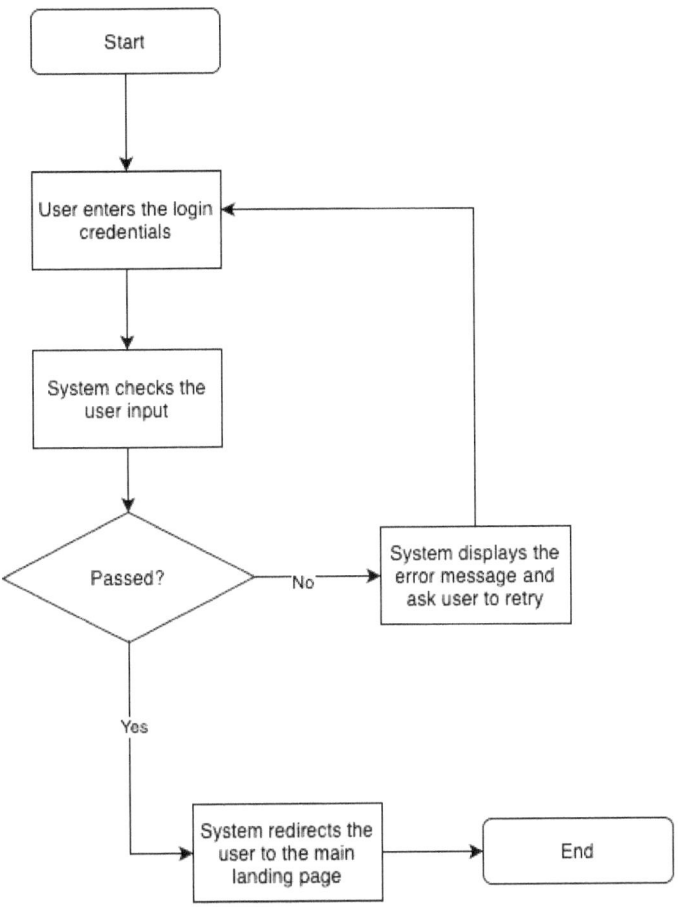

This is just the basic construct of a simple flow diagram. There are more components that can be used in the diagram, for instance, shape to display processes, input/output and many more.

Sample diagram 2:

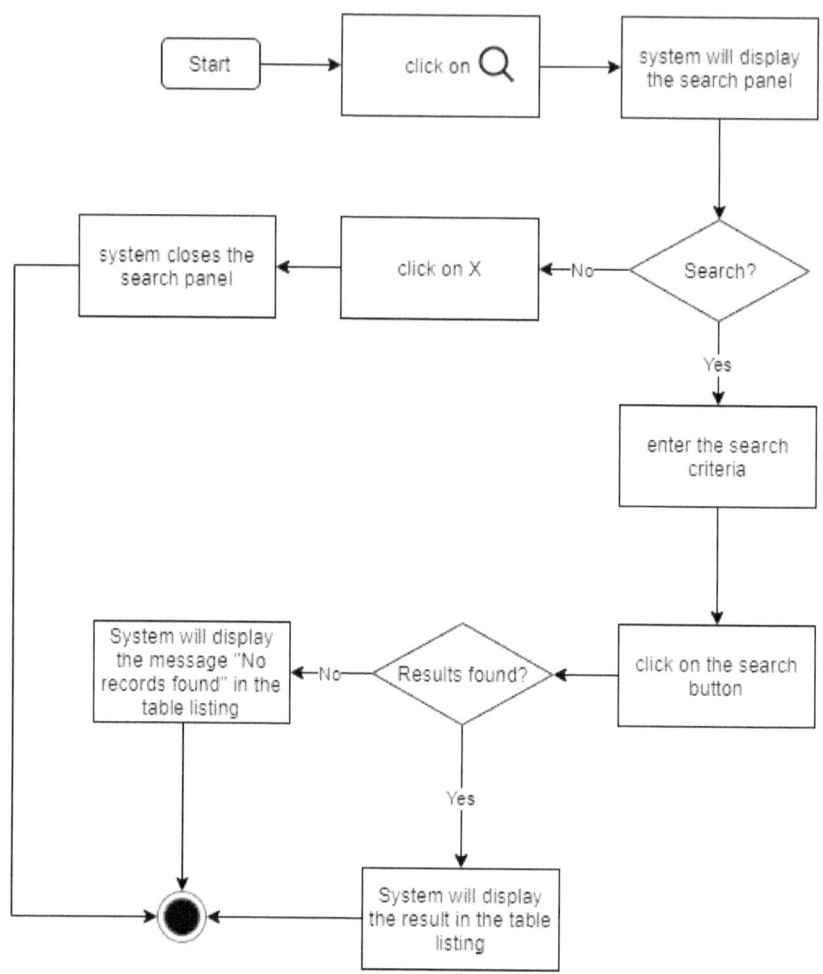

Try to understand the flow above and describe it as an exercise.

The use of storyboarding and prototypes

Storyboarding is a great way to provide visualisation on what the end product will look like. What it does is to convert the process flow diagram into a step by step screen or a dummy prototype so that end users and developers alike can look at how the system will work. By having the expectations set, it will help to remove a lot of uncertainties during the development phase where changes requested later often cause delays in projects. Storyboarding serves as a great method to engage business users identifying the user experience they want from the system, and to get them to review if the proposal can sufficiently address their issues and concerns.

Tips:
Depending on the the completeness of the screens, if you have enough screens to actually let users to go through all the features and functions, along with the mock results (or even the mock warning messages if the users perform the actions that warrant for such messages), you will be able to lock down the deliverables for the users. Any new changes that come after the sign off will be treated as a change request that can be worked on at a later stage. The screens can later be reused for other projects with similar requirements which can be modified easily for presentations later on.

Tools that can help with storyboarding:

- AXURE Rapid Prototyping

- Web Flow
- Adobe XD
- Invision Studio
- Adobe Photoshop/Illustrator
- Sketch
- Figma

And of course, the good old

- Microsoft Powerpoint

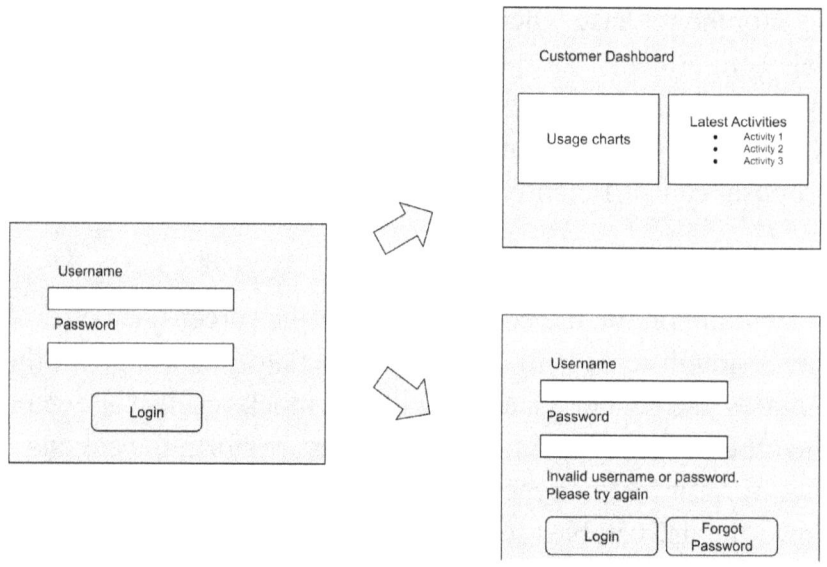

Sample screen flow for a user login process

Functional and Non-Functional requirements.

Understanding the difference between functional and non-functional requirements.

"What are non-functional requirements? Do we need to put in the non-functional requirements in that document? Aren't those the developer's job to figure out?" These are some of the questions I get from the business analysts. Most of them never consider the aspects of non-functional requirements when preparing the solution or proposal for the business users. Many more did not even know what non-functional requirements are. They only focus on the functional requirements and ignore the non-functional requirements for most of the part. While we can still meet the expectations by delivering the solution with all the functional requirements, it might not provide the best user experience to the business users.

So what are functional and nonfunctional requirements?

Functional Requirements

Functional requirements are the requirements that are mandatory as part of the solution or it will not meet the objective of the project as laid out by the business users. In other words, the system or solution will fail since functional requirements are the core features that are required for the system or solution to run successfully. In other words, function requirements form the key objectives of the solution design. Failing to complete and deliver all the functional requirements may result in the project roll out failure as business users might reject the solution later on for not meeting their business objectives.

Functional requirements usually provide the details and the expectations for each business problem that the project will have to address. Business analysts will often create the use cases along with the response to each input and set the expected output.

Examples of requirements that are considered as functional requirements:

- A required feature for the users, e.g. report generation
- Business rules and processes that must be met
- Compliance and data integrity checks
- Integration requirements
- Transactions that must be tracked
- Expected data input and output

Non-functional Requirements

Non-functional requirements are requirements that need to be in place in order to deliver a specific function. They are not as vital as the functional requirements since not having them will not make a system fail. However non-functional requirements are important in ensuring that the system delivered will provide an overall good experience to the business users. Non-functional requirements generally do not dictate the functionalities of a system but they will affect how the function will perform in the system. Ignoring non-functional requirements too much will create a system with horrible user experience and rack up the technical debts.

Examples of non-functional requirements:

- System uptime and availability
- The acceptable time for a function to run, e.g. the speed of the report generation
- The maximum number of transactions that can be loaded a a time, which will impact the performance of the system, and subsequently affecting the user experience
- Usability of the system. Is the design easy for users to navigate and perform the required functions?

Sometimes it can be confusing in defining and categorising a requirement into functional and non-functional requirements. Here's a summary:

Functional Requirements	Non-functional Requirements
Defines the features and functions of the system	Defines the requirements that mostly affects the performance of the system

Details the rules and processes on how the system should work	Details the way how the system will behave
Usually stand-alone functions that are required by the business users.	Having dependencies on the requirements from the business users.
Essential to the system	Desirable but not essential
Can be defined into clear use cases	Can be defined as a quality attribute
Obvious to the business users	Non-obvious to the business users but will impact the user experience

Good communication is key for a good business analyst

A good business analyst will need to be equipped with fantastic communication skills since they will be spending a good amount of time talking to people around them; from the stakeholders to the developers and even the project sponsors. They need to be able to understand and interpret what the stakeholders needed and communicate correctly on the expectations back to the developers. Bad communication will often leave out much crucial information that might be detrimental to the success of a project. I have seen many cases where communication was so bad that it misled the developers on the customer's expectation and they had to redo the project from scratch, wasting all the time, effort, money and most importantly reputation of the company. There was a case where the client got so frustrated at communicating their needs to the business analyst that the client started dialling the number of the head of the Research and Development department directly to resolve their issues, all because the business analyst in charge couldn't understand their problems and their needs. The client demanded to change the business analyst for the project or the company risked having the project terminated.

"We all have seen the game where five people had to wear headphones, with the first person having to describe the word to the next and the last person having to get it right. If all of them are able to communicate and understand perfectly, then

the correct message is sent across. Otherwise, it will be a disaster for the last person."

Good communication skills will also help to foster better relationships with the business users and developers alike. Business users are able to build their trust in you if you are able to communicate effectively and efficiently with them. They will feel confident that their message gets to you and your development team which will then be translated accurately in the solution design. Once they have the trust in you, it will be fairly easy to negotiate any business requirements or even project related stuff, e.g. the job scope, feature set and other issues with the customers. They will be more willing to accept your feedback and justification on items like project timeline, effort required and changes to their original request since you have proven to them that you are trustworthy enough to handle their projects. I have had clients changing their operation process to suit our software process because during our discussions, I have demonstrated and communicated the key benefits of using our software solutions, along with the analysis of the clients' issues and how our solution resolves those problems. I had even pointed out the root cause and reason that they are having high operation costs were due to their ineffective business process. In the end, both parties agreed that our software process had the more efficient way of doing things. They are willing to give our software a try and it ended up improving their business process and saving their operation expenditure. On our side, we spent very little effort in customising and delivering the solution to them. Win-win situation I would say, which is the best outcome in this relationship.

"Communication is a two way process. You need to understand the customer's requirements but at the same time, get them to understand what you are offering."

It can be frightening for new business analysts to start talking to clients, especially the demanding and difficult-to-deal-with-type that will ask for unreasonable requirements with a ridiculous deadline. Some business users might force the new, green, business analysts to listen to them, just because they have been working in this industry longer, albeit having longer working years does not grant the person knowledge in solution design unless the business user is one with a strong technical background.

Usually a senior business analyst or the project manager will take the lead in the discussions, like the project kick off, requirement gathering workshops, leaving the rest of the tasks such as interviews, Q&A etc to the business analyst to handle. However, I have seen too many incidents where the project manager will just attend the first meeting, and throw the poor, junior business analyst to deal with the business users. Some of them were traumatised with the incidents, causing most of them to repeat the cycle to the next batch of newcomers. I was one of them to go through this unfortunate event when my manager disappeared the next day. I have had to take over and communicate with the business user directly since then.

Tips at work:
If you happen to have such a shitty manager that landed you in the same predicament, either bring it up to your HR on this incident, or talk to your manager or another senior if you have this issue. Get them to place you under a senior that can guide

you so that you can start picking up the tasks and become independent eventually. When you are at a stage where you are able to handle things on your own, you can start offering guidance to your junior.

However, If all channels fail, it is time to look out for better prospects because knowledge and experience takes time to build. Wasting time learning nothing won't do you any good in climbing the career ladder.

How can I improve my communication skills?

As for the business analysts, there are many ways that one can improve on the communication skills:

Be confident – a person with good confidence is usually seen as more reliable and trustworthy. If you speak with confidence and high certainty, clients will be more willing to listen and trust your judgement. However, you will need to ensure that you deliver what you have communicated with them or they will think of you as nothing more than empty talk which will erode their confidence in you. You might be nervous when speaking to a new stranger that you have never met before. Show respect and politeness when dealing with new people to create a good impression.

Talk on the same wavelength - Build your domain knowledge that clients can resonate with you. It is important for both parties to have the same understanding. Without this, clients will begin to feel doubtful that you are able to understand their current problems and concerns, which could then create a bad impression that you will not be able to deliver a good solution to them. If you and your clients have difficulties understanding one another, try to understand them first by listening to their views and opinions before making any judgement or conclusions, unless you are very sure that what you are proposing will definitely solve their problem. Otherwise, it is good to hear them out first, analyse their concerns and proceed from there.

Be respectful – Always be respectful to those that you are communicating with regardless of their position. A junior finance clerk deserves the same amount of respect as a Chief Finance Officer. Imagine if your client is being rude to you because you are still a junior business analyst or because they think "customer is always right". As long as the person you are talking to does not behave like a total arsehole, then everyone deserves the same respect. Furthermore, building good rapport with the lower level staff is beneficial as they are most likely the ones who understand most of the current issues that you need to solve for their company. If you have good relationships with them, they will be able to assist and support your proposal which their management will definitely get feedback from them after your presentation.

Ask questions, but not the stupid ones – One of my lecturers back then said this before, "There are no stupid questions, just the bad ones." He was trying to encourage us to ask questions on any topics of our interests. But we must understand and prepare the questions beforehand, otherwise he will ignore them and penalise us in a funny way. No one likes to deal with someone who comes unprepared. It is a waste of time for the clients since they will have to explain the basics which they will definitely expect you to already have the answers for or having done your research prior to meeting them. There was one junior business analyst who kept asking bad questions until the client banned him from future discussions. For example, instead of asking "What is the invoice process?", one should ask "How did you process your invoice?", and then proceed to provide some examples of a generic invoice process to identify the differences. In this way, your client will know that you do have some knowledge in this area and you will be able to map the key differences instantly with suggestions to solve their problems, all in the same discussion, rather than having them to explain the entire invoicing process to you.

Use infographics to support your presentation – Having these materials will help to bring across your idea easily to the clients since it will help them to digest your key points as long as the content is short, precise and straight to the point. Any additional information can be communicated verbally to them. This will allow an open discussion if there are use cases that are not present in the slides. Having long, convoluted slides will only cause everyone to lose focus in the discussion as everyone will have trouble trying to digest the content on the slides, rather than having a meaningful discussion on the business requirements or proposals. Apart from that, you will be showing a higher degree of professionalism if you can always prepare some useful slides before any discussion. Clients usually appreciate the extra effort. When they ask for the meeting summary, you can just add the missing points to the deck and send it to them, saving you time to remember and write down what was discussed previously.

Practice makes perfect – No one is good at something from the start. It takes tremendous training and preparation to master every skill. So in order to communicate well, start building the courage and confidence when talking to strangers. You can start by striking up some conversation with your local bartender, your hairstylist, that friendly barista etc. Start socialising around your neighbourhood or at the gym. If you find it difficult, or are even terrified at the idea of speaking to a stranger, then you will encounter much difficulty taking up the role as a business analyst as this role requires one to master the art of communication in order to better discuss and negotiate with the clients on their needs.

Tips: Ways to "fish" for information and user feedback

Let's say you are in a situation where you are working on a project where you are not the domain expert and it is difficult to get any information online.

In this scenario, what can you do to work with the users to get more data required for the proposal?

1. Try establishing relevant use cases and build follow up questions with the business user

The pain points and issues that are plaguing the users might be similar to the past projects that you have worked on. Try digging into your memory files and share them with the users. Otherwise, try researching online on what is the generic process flow, common issues and desired features for clients in this industry. Some industries, e.g. financial, have similar processes and business rules since they are regulated by authorities. Therefore it is always a good idea to study beforehand on the industry of your clients before meeting them for a discussion.

Always prepare follow up questions or ask them ad hoc to start gathering those feedback from business users. If needed, you can use a recorder to store all the conversations for later use when you are linking up all the information while preparing your proposal. However, do remember to inform the users if you are using a recorder as some might not feel comfortable with that approach. Some of the business users do not like being recorded in meetings, so look for alternatives to get your meeting minutes. Now there are AI assisted tools out there that can be integrated with the meeting conference software that can help to summarise the meeting key points. You just need to be creative!

We love to connect with people that share the same wavelength with us. The same logic applies to our clients and business users. If you are able to build a good relationship with them, you can actually learn more about the business operations from them, some which the top management might not even know.

2. Common sense

Use common sense to ask relevant questions to the users. Having illogical questions will put you in a bad light as an incompetent business analyst. Customers are paying good money for the projects and they would be expecting someone with critical thinking skills to help them solve the problem, and not some annoying twat that kept asking questions that make no sense.

So ask questions like these,

Why are they using this method and not the other method that is seemingly more efficient?

Are we able to generalise or standardise the process? If not, why?

I have read that the eKYC process has to capture all these landmarks in order to pass the check. Your process captures less landmarks, is there a reason for that?

I see that your process might not be complied with the regulations set by the monetary authorities. May I know if you are granted the exception? Otherwise we will have to include this in the business requirements to make sure that you are fully complied with the rules and regulations.

These questions will help to open up more details on why the company is getting into the problems that they are facing, and they can be the source of input when you are designing your solution so that it will be more relevant to address their concerns. Most important of all, asking good questions will avoid offending the clients which some may take it personally. In addition to that, you can use the same information to tick off those ideas that you have which they might have tried them before and they did not work for them. You will save a lot of time and effort if you are able to skip those.

Avoid asking questions like these,

What is a landmark in eKYC?

How come yours is called criteria and not a landmark?

Is your process regulated under the monetary authorities?

How come your process is so bad? Did you come up with this?

What do you need?

Clients and business users usually feel annoyed if the business analysts handling their projects did not do some homework beforehand since they are expecting a great deal from someone who will be acting as a consultant for them. Also, they would want to learn from your past successful projects in order to map against their own set processes and operations.

Let them lead along and then drill down into the fine details to better focus and project scope definition. Having an open question will just get users to throw everything at you, including the nice to have features that will generate little value for the project.

3. Build the trust with your users

Once you have built the trust with the stakeholders, clients or the business users, they will be more comfortable in sharing crucial or sensitive information with you. Communication with them will become easier and they might even help to defend you in some difficult meetings with other business users, or even from your own boss.

I have had that experience where the business users defended me when my former project manager tried to get credit by sabotaging my presentation. The business users just ganged up and destroyed her questions aiming to paint my proposal as not something that the business users want. But it backfired, more so in front of the directors and the bosses of the company. True story.

4. Some mind reading skills would be helpful

If you are born with mind reading skills, then you already have an advantage with jobs that require frequent communications with customers. Otherwise, you might need to develop some skills in reading the facial expressions and gestures of the business users as the expressions do convey information that they might have difficulty uttering out. They might frown if your solution is not what they are expecting, or they might lean forward if they show interest in what you are proposing at the moment. Having the ability to capture these gestures or signs will give you better control over the discussion such as:

Should you go further with your ideas? or should you stop since the idea might not be what they are looking for. The key is to have a fruitful discussion in every session. Oh and also, please plan out the next step and email the users the agenda in the upcoming meetings. Nobody likes wasting time in meetings with no objectives, well except those bosses with no better things to do at the office.

5. Having good analytical skills

To be successful as a business analyst, you will need to have strong analytical skills. How do you develop one? Developing a good analytical skill usually involves a mix of habits, techniques, and practices. You will always need to:

1. **Cultivate Curiosity**: Always ask questions and seek to understand how things work. This mindset helps you dig deeper into problems and find underlying patterns.

2. **Practise Critical Thinking**: Evaluate information from multiple perspectives. Challenge assumptions and consider alternative explanations.

3. **Break Problems Down**: Divide complex problems into smaller, more manageable parts. Analyse each part individually before putting them together to understand the whole picture.

4. **Enhance Your Data Skills**: Get comfortable working with data. Learn how to interpret data sets, recognise trends, and use statistical tools. Tools like Excel, SQL or Python can be very helpful. It will be great if you pick up skills to use tools like Tableau, PowerBI, Google Analytics etc to help with your data analysis.

5. **Improve Your Problem-Solving Techniques**: Work on developing structured approaches to problem-solving, such as the scientific method or root cause analysis.

6. **Learn from Examples**: Study case studies, analyses, and solutions from others in your field. Understand how they approached problems and what strategies they used. If you are new to the job, the information are at your fingertips. All you need to do is to enter relevant keywords in the google search box or even ask ChatGPT about it. However, do process the information and not take them as correct and relevant for your projects.

7. **Develop Attention to Detail**: Pay close attention to the details of the information you're working with. Small details can often lead to significant insights.

By incorporating these practices into your routine, you can develop sharper analytical skills and improve your ability to tackle complex problems effectively.

Some other information gathering techniques:

- Verbal surveys and feedback
- Tickets and complaints received from users
- Brainstorming sessions
- Usage statistics and preference

How to conduct a workshop and workshops for requirement gathering

Conducting a workshop for requirement gathering is a crucial step in ensuring that you capture the needs, expectations, and constraints of all stakeholders involved in a project. Here's a structured approach to running such a workshop effectively:

Preparation

1. Define Objectives:

Clearly outline the goals of the workshop. What specific requirements are you aiming to gather? What problems are you trying to solve?

2. Identify Stakeholders:

Determine who should attend the workshop. This might include project sponsors, end-users, subject matter experts, and other relevant parties.

3. Choose the Right Facilitator:

Select someone who is skilled in leading discussions and managing group dynamics. This could be an internal team member or an external consultant.

4. Prepare Materials:

Gather any documents or background information that participants might need. Prepare slides, templates, and other resources that will help facilitate the discussion.

5. **Set an Agenda:**

    Create a detailed agenda that includes time slots for each topic or activity. Ensure that there's a balance between presentations, discussions, and hands-on activities.

6. **Logistics:**

    Book a suitable venue if in-person, or set up a virtual meeting space if online. Ensure all necessary equipment (projectors, whiteboards, etc.) is available and functioning.

During the Workshop

1. **Introduction:**

    Start by introducing yourself, the purpose of the workshop, and the agenda. Make sure everyone knows each other and understands their roles.

2. **Establish Ground Rules:**

Set some ground rules for participation, such as one person speaking at a time, being respectful of differing opinions, and staying on topic.

3. **Gather Requirements:**

    Use a mix of techniques to elicit requirements:
    - **Brainstorming:** Encourage participants to freely share ideas.
    - **Interviews:** Ask specific questions to individuals or groups.
    - **Surveys/Questionnaires:** Use pre-prepared questions to gather information.
    - **Use Cases and Scenarios:** Describe specific situations to understand requirements in context.
    - **User Stories:** Have participants describe what they want from the system in simple, end-user terms.
    - **Affinity Diagrams:** Group similar ideas or requirements to identify common themes.

4. **Facilitate Discussion:**

    Guide discussions to ensure that all viewpoints are considered and that the conversation remains productive and focused.

5. **Document Findings:**

Capture all requirements, ideas, and discussions in real time. Use tools like whiteboards, sticky notes, or digital documentation platforms.

6. **Prioritise Requirements:**

    Work with participants to prioritise requirements based on factors such as importance, feasibility, and impact.

7. **Review and Validate:**

    Summarise the key points and confirm with participants that the captured requirements accurately reflect their needs and expectations.

Post-Workshop

1. **Compile and Organize:**

    Organise the notes and documentation into a structured format. This might include a requirements specification document or a backlog of user stories.

2. **Distribute Findings:**

    Share the compiled requirements with all participants and relevant stakeholders for review and confirmation.

3. **Follow-Up:**

Address any additional questions or clarifications that arise after the workshop. Schedule follow-up meetings if necessary to finalise requirements.

4. **Feedback:**

    Gather feedback on the workshop process to identify areas for improvement in future workshops.

By following these steps, you can ensure that your requirement gathering workshops are productive and yield comprehensive, actionable insights for your project.

Habits that a Business Analyst Need to Avoid

1. Setting ridiculous expectations without first consulting with the technical team before agreeing to the stakeholders

This is one of the traps that many business analysts fall into. I get many complaints from the developers that the business analyst or the project manager went on and agreed on ridiculous deadlines and forced the developers to deliver within the timeframe before first consulting with them. Imagine if the developers asked the business analysts to complete a FRS that will run into hundreds of pages in three days without understanding the scope and details of the entire requirements. Furthermore, business analysts will often have to revise the requirements documents after reviewing and discussing with the clients. The point I am trying to make is that every job has its roles and responsibilities that come along with the expertise required for that job. We should never answer on behalf of those before consulting and getting their feedback, especially if they will be the one doing the job. Ignoring them is not only disrespectful to them, it will cause unnecessary delays and frustration from the team members. Imagine setting a 15 minute time frame for a heart surgeon for your operation that requires at least 2 hours. This will only put tremendous pressure on the person working on it and usually result in low quality work being delivered because they need to meet the ridiculous deadline committed by you. The heart surgeon might just cut one of your arteries and call it a day if he needs to complete the surgery in 15 minutes, leaving you either having a long term heart defect, or worse, 6 feet under.

"We always have to do what customers are asking." These were the words from my project manager when I was still a business analyst at that time, something I disagree with. Yes, we have to deliver the "expectations" of the customer, a solution that will solve their problems within a reasonable time frame and not commit to a deadline where they will end up with a bad system full of bugs. We want happy customers, not the angry and disappointed ones. But many customers love to put pressure on the business analysts to get them deliver the job in a short period of time, so they could save some money if the charges are based effort, e.g. <x> amount per man day, which unfortunately many of the business analysts seem to oblige, so they can please the customers. Yet, they failed to recognise the consequences from such actions if they screw it up; angry customers for getting crap quality software, and a frustrated team that is constantly put under pressure. A lose-lose situation for all parties.

A good business analyst will need to balance out the scope against the project time frame set by the project manager. They will have to get the feedback from the developers on the effort required for a feature or a solution, then review the feedback with the project manager so that a more accurate project timeline or scope could be agreed with the customers. Wrong expectations will only lead to bad impressions from the clients which would lower the trustworthiness of your company as a whole. Therefore, being able to prepare good requirements documents and having excellent communication skills could be helpful in reducing time wastage in a project, which was one of the main causes for the delay in a project.

Having said that, this does not mean business analysts will have to take in the effort or time needed to complete a feature from the developers as it is. They will still need to meet the project timeline set by the project manager, at most with reasonable delays if circumstances prevent that. I have encountered developers who would exaggerate the effort needed for a small change, maybe just 1 to 2 lines of code change but they asked for three days to complete the task. Business analysts who have the technical knowledge would be more advantageous when dealing with this type of scenario. They usually have a rough idea on how long it will take for a change, since they were developers before. They can always seek justification from the developers if required. For those who did not have such an advantage, you could get a second opinion from the technical lead or other developers. If your gut feeling is telling you that the developer might be giving too much buffer time for the task, get them to break down the effort and verify it with the technical lead. If this is handled well, developers will know that they will not be able to give you a bullshit time frame for a simple task and you will provide the customers with a more accurate expectation.

2. Did not have the correct domain knowledge for the job

Many business analysts did not have the required knowledge when they just started their job. This is perfectly understandable and is completely normal. No one understands rocket science the day they were born. I recalled the times when I was still a junior business analyst at a software company where I had very little experience in the industries of the clients that the company is serving. I had to pick up new knowledge depending on the project that I was assigned to. I was involved in the hotel booking system for some time until suddenly I was asked to work on a casino management system for a well known casino. The worst thing about it was that after I got the assignment, I was flown to the client's office and the very next day, I had to present what I know about the casino's business process and ways to digitise the casino's operation. At that time, I had zero, yes, zero knowledge on how casinos work since all I had was the knowledge of hotel booking systems. I only had one night before meeting all the director-level stakeholders. There were no guidance from the seniors. I was thrown into this project alone. The only thing I could do at that time was to read up everything about casino operations on Wikipedia, learning all the keywords and definition, so that I have sufficient knowledge to respond or ask the correct questions. There was no ChatGPT that I could rely on back then. If I went in without doing so, it would be a nightmare and the client for sure will be sending in complaints to my HR for sending in an idiot to deal with them.

Not knowing about something is fine, but not trying to understand just shows that you are not serious about your job. - from my mentor that had helped me tremendously in my career.

Always do your research on the topics before you start talking to the business users or stakeholders. From there you will be able to understand how their business works, their common problems and pain points, then relate those issues with their current operation. The discussion with them will be more engaging once both parties are speaking the same language, or tuned to the same wavelength. When you are able to have meaningful conversations with the clients, you will start building trust with them.

The common problem with some junior business analysts was they relied too much on the seniors or other developers to solve the problem for them. It is very easy for business analysts to act just as a messenger and throw all the problems to others to solve for them. Failure to learn new things means you failed your job as a business analyst. This role requires someone who can use the knowledge and experience from past projects and apply them to similar projects. The role also requires the business analyst to be creative in drafting solutions to the clients as different organisations would have different sets of problems.

3. Always make assumptions and not check with the relevant stakeholders

We often make assumptions without checking with stakeholders due to a combination of convenience, cognitive biases, and communication challenges. Assumptions can simplify decision-making and speed up processes, particularly when faced with time constraints or incomplete information. Cognitive biases, such as overconfidence or confirmation bias, can lead us to rely on our own judgments rather than seeking validation. Additionally, communication barriers, such as lack of stakeholder availability or ineffective communication channels, may discourage direct engagement. While assumptions can seem practical, they risk misaligning with actual needs and creating costly issues later, making thorough stakeholder consultation crucial for accurate and successful outcomes.

As such, avoid the pitfalls of making assumptions in requirement gathering, always engage relevant stakeholders from the start, using open-ended questions to explore their needs and expectations. Validate and document their input clearly, and regularly revisit and refine requirements through iterative feedback. Employ various techniques like interviews, surveys, and prototypes to cross-check information and ensure accuracy. By actively involving stakeholders and continuously confirming details, you can ensure that requirements are precise, well-understood, and aligned with the project's objectives.

4. Reject the requirements upfront without proper communication

Never reject the requirements from stakeholders immediately. If the requirement is not feasible, try to justify or explain the logic behind in order to persuade them to change their mind. If they insist, inform them that the requirement will be included in the backlog and come back to them for clarifications. If they are the difficult type of person to deal with, e.g. wants to have the requirement implemented immediately, try to check with their superior if you have the access to them, or escalate it to your own superior to assist you in dealing with them. Never burn the bridge or harm the relationships with the stakeholders as this won't be your first project with the, Having a good relationship with the stakeholders will allow you to gain useful knowledge into the industry, e.g. Business operations, processes, industry know-how etc which you can leverage and use them for your next project.

Can anyone be a Business Analyst?

Well yes. It is the same with any other job. Anyone can be a programmer as well if they are interested in programming. I have met many very good programmers that came from a financial background or having a law degree. Anyone can be good at their job as long as they have the motivation and passion for it as practice makes perfect. Since we spend most of our time at our jobs, it makes perfect sense to find one that fits your career aspirations and is enjoyable at the same time.

The most important question that one should ask oneself before taking up a job as a business analyst is that:

Do I have what it takes to be a great business analyst?

A programmer will need to keep up with the technology and apply them appropriately on a solution.
A business analyst will need to gain enough industry knowledge and apply them appropriately to address the clients' business issues.

These two roles are equally important in a project setup. I have seen many developers saying that they can be a better business analyst than the ones they are working with at the moment. While in some cases it might be true, this also shows that they did not have the chance to work with a good business analyst. Some of those developers later found themselves unable to deliver their job as a business analyst after trying it out as they design the solution from a developer's perspective, rather than designing a solution from the clients' perspective.

The role requires different attention, qualities and criteria as compared to the qualities required for a good programmer. See the qualities in the previous chapter.

Career Progression of a Business Analyst role

This is another question that I get asked many times by juniors or those who are interested in taking up the role as a business analyst. There are many paths that one could take after a few successful years in this role. Your domain and business knowledge that you have built up over the years plays a vital role. Coupled with strong communication skills, here are some common career progression for a business analyst, after the progression as a Senior Business Analyst.

- **Project Manager** - Many senior business analysts are usually promoted to the role of a project manager since they understand well on the projects that they have done or are currently working on. Furthermore, they have developed good connections with the existing clients through the various projects. Having all these experiences and client relationships allows the business analyst to deal with the customers easily since they understand the clients' behaviour and how they operate.

- **Product Manager** - Experience and knowledge are key assets for a product manager. Having those past experiences as a business analyst are useful for a person to take up the role as a product manager as he or she will understand the common issues and pain points faced by the business users from the same industry and how to solve them since they have tried out the solution in actual projects for previous clients. This will allow the product manager to design a product or a solution that will be in demand by the targeted users.

- **Consultant** - Strong communication skills, creative and having in-depth business and technical knowledge will help a business analyst transition into a consultant role easily since a consultant must be well equipped with all these qualities to help solve the customer's problems and deliver value to them.

What I would suggest will be the following sequence for better progression, of course you can adjust it according to your needs.

Business Analyst > Senior Business Analyst > Project Manager > Product Manager > Senior Product Manager > Head of Product/Consultant > Chief Product Officer or CEO

For me it is a bit risky to jump directly into the product manager role after spending just one year or less as a business analyst. I had a few juniors that were promoted to the product manager role after spending 6 months as a business analyst as the company needed more product managers at that time. It turned out to be a nightmare as the company received numerous complaints on the new products designed by these juniors. In fact we had to kill off a few products because they weren't able to solve the customers' problems and provide value to them despite all the fancy bells and whistles that came with the product. Ultimately, clients will want to have a product that can resolve their pain points and benefit their business, not "nice-to-have" functions that serve nothing more than a gimmick. It might impress them at first, but in the long term, it will only bring more harm to the reputation of the product when the complaints start piling up.

If you are a business analyst and have some other roles in mind, and you think you have the skills and qualities to do it well, feel free to explore the role. This is just a quick guide to show what a business analyst can do after having accumulated all the knowledge and experiences over the years.

Will Artificial Intelligence (AI) replace the role of a business analyst

Well the answer is yes and no. It really depends on the industry and the scale of projects or the companies that you are working in.

In an era dominated by rapid technological advancements, the question of whether AI will replace human roles, including that of the business analyst, looms large. While AI undoubtedly has the potential to revolutionise how business analysis is conducted, a closer examination reveals that its role is likely to be one of augmentation rather than outright replacement.

AI is adept at automating repetitive tasks like data collection, data analysis, and generating reports. It can quickly process vast amounts of data to identify patterns and trends, which can help business users make more informed decisions when they are preparing the business requirement documents. In fact, if the AI tool is capable of helping the business users to prepare proper business requirement documents based on the past projects, then there is little need for a business analyst to act as an intermediary between the business users and the development team. The business users can communicate directly with the development team by getting AI to formulate the requirements for them.

Despite its impressive capabilities, AI faces significant limitations that prevent it from fully replacing human business analysts. One such limitation is the lack of contextual understanding. While AI can analyse structured data effectively, it often struggles with unstructured or qualitative data and may fail to grasp the nuanced complexities of human interactions and business environments.

Furthermore, creativity and innovation, integral aspects of business analysis, remain firmly within the realm of human expertise. While AI can identify existing patterns and trends, it lacks the capacity for imaginative thinking and problem-solving. Business analysts frequently leverage their creativity to devise novel solutions and strategies tailored to specific organisational challenges, a task that AI is ill-equipped to perform.

Moreover, domain expertise, honed through years of experience and immersion in a particular industry or sector, distinguishes human analysts from their AI counterparts. Business analysis often requires a deep understanding of industry dynamics, market trends, regulatory frameworks, and customer behaviour, insights that are cultivated through human observation and interaction.

Communication and stakeholder management represent another area where human analysts hold a distinct advantage. Effective communication is essential for bridging gaps between different stakeholders, facilitating collaboration, and translating technical insights into actionable recommendations. AI lacks the interpersonal skills and emotional intelligence required for such interactions, making human analysts indispensable in fostering productive relationships within organisations.

Ethical and moral judgement, critical components of decision-making in business analysis, also elude AI. Complex ethical dilemmas, such as those arising from privacy concerns, data governance, and social responsibility, demand nuanced human judgement informed by ethical principles and values. AI algorithms, devoid of moral reasoning, are ill-suited to navigate these ethical intricacies.

In conclusion, while AI has the potential to augment various aspects of business analysis, it is unlikely to fully replace human business analysts. The integration of AI-driven tools and technologies will undoubtedly reshape the landscape of business analysis, enhancing efficiency, accuracy, and insights generation. However, the unique blend of human skills, including contextual understanding, creativity, domain expertise, communication, and ethical judgement, ensures that the role of the business analyst remains indispensable in driving strategic decision-making and organisational success. Thus, rather than fearing obsolescence, business analysts should embrace AI as a powerful ally in their quest to deliver value and drive innovation in an increasingly complex business environment.

In other words, human business analysts should utilise the power of technology as a powerful research tool to improve on the work quality, speed of delivery and gain more knowledge which will help them to be a better business analyst in the long run.

Interview tips for a Business Analyst role

If you are still interested in landing yourself in this role, there are a few tips that the hiring managers might be looking out for when they are interviewing the candidates (that is if the manager has the skills, otherwise you can just bullshit your way through. True story. But trust me, you will never want to work under such managers if you get hired.

For me, when I am hiring a new business analysts, I generally look at few items, depending on their job experience:

For juniors, I will first check their communication skills, both in writing and verbal. This is to test if the candidate is able to interpret and create accurate documentation to deliver the message across as intended. Lower scores will be given if the candidate demonstrated poor understanding or committed too many errors when communicating the message.

The next skill that I will be looking for is the basic understanding on how a system behaves, especially in the IT industry. If the candidate demonstrates sufficient understanding of the system design, then he will score better than those who do not. You will need to have some relatable experience when applying for a job as it will cost companies to train and get the staff ready. So usually hiring managers will get someone with the experience so that they can put them to work in the shortest period of time. However, there are exceptions to that; if a candidate is showing great passion and is able to quickly pick up the knowledge, he or she will be considered. This shows that the candidate is worth being invested in training that can contribute better in the future.

After that, it will be the problem solving test where the candidate is given some problems or use cases to propose a solution to resolve as many of the issues raised. The candidate will have to demonstrate the ability to adapt to different scenarios according to the business cases and suggest changes or solutions to each of the cases mentioned. Since business operations change frequently, candidates who are highly adaptable to changes, having good problem solving skills and creativity will have a better advantage against others who demonstrate poorly in this area.

For seniors, or those looking at a more senior role, I will get them to walk me through on the processes that they have used in the past projects and their decisions of going with the design that ended up in the final product, apart from the tests given to the juniors mentioned above, to better understand how they will be managing the project, and if the methods used were effective. Senior business analysts will often be depended on to make difficult decisions in deciding the requirements that the developers will be working on. Having said that, the most important skill in a business analyst, or in any role, is common sense. This is a vital skill if one were to excel in his or her job. It helps to create sensible solutions that will have a balance in everything; features that will solve the problems and bring business values within a reasonable timeline and costs. If you have good common sense, you are already in the lead for the competition.

Hope the tips above assist you in some ways if you are applying for a business analyst role.

Good luck!

About the Author

Kyle C. is an entrepreneur, investor, and middle-class worker who has worked with various companies across different regions around the world. Equipped with his knowledge, he began his life as an amateur writer to produce some writings based on his personal experiences so that he could share his stories with a wider audience as compared to a selected few among his circle of friends.

Other books by this Author:

1. *Layman's Guide to Investing, with a bit of common sense (2020)*
2. *How to Get Rich, by understanding the economy (2020)*
3. *Words for Humanity (2020)*
4. *My Weight Loss Journey, Without Spending a Single Dime (2021)*
5. *How to Create A Good Product (2021)*
6. *You Should Start Thinking About Yourself, For Once (2021)*
7. *Why I Have No Savings & How to Start Saving Up (2021)*
8. *How to become a Great Business Analyst (2022)*
9. *14 Ghost Short Stories (2022)*
10. *Our Deepest Desire In Life - Freedom (2022)*
11. *How to become a Sales Grand Master (2022)*
12. *How to Be an Exceptional Manager: Everything You Need to Know In Mastering the Art of Management (2023)*
13. *Wisdom's Whisper - Quotations to Guide and Inspire Your Journey (2024)*

www.ingramcontent.com/pod-product-compliance
Lightning Source LLC
Chambersburg PA
CBHW070358230526
45471CB00006B/2628